My Emotions Through Emojis

FEELING AMUSED

BY
THEIA LAKE

Enslow
PUBLISHING

Please visit our website, www.enslow.com.
For a free color catalog of all our high-quality books, call toll free 1-800-398-2504 or fax 1-877-980-4454.

Cataloging-in-Publication Data
Names: Lake, Theia.
Title: Feeling amused / Theia Lake.
Description: New York : Enslow Publishing, 2024. | Series: My emotions through emojis | Includes index.
Identifiers: ISBN 9781978533301 (pbk.) | ISBN 9781978533318 (library bound) | ISBN 9781978533325 (ebook)
Subjects: LCSH: Humor in children–Juvenile literature. | Laughter–Juvenile literature.
Classification: LCC BF575.L3 L35 2023 | DDC 152.4'3–dc23

Published in 2024 by
Enslow Publishing
2544 Clinton Street
Buffalo, NY 14224

Designer: Tanya Dellaccio Keeney
Editor: Theresa Emminizer

Photo credits: Cover (phone) Victor Z/Shutterstock.com; cover, series art (clouds) Theus/Shutterstock.com; cover, series art (emojis) stas11/Shutterstock.com; p. 5 TY Lim/Shutterstock.com; p. 7 fizkes/Shutterstock.com; p. 9 wavebreakmedia/Shutterstock.com; pp. 11, 13 greenland/Shutterstock.com; p. 15 Roman Samborskyi/Shutterstock.com; pp. 17, 19 LightField Studios/Shutterstock.com; p. 21 Monkey Business Images/Shutterstock.com.

Printed in the United States of America

CPSIA compliance information: Batch #CS24ENS: For further information contact Enslow Publishing, at 1-800-398-2504.

CONTENTS

Boldface words appear in Words to Know.

ARE YOU AMUSED?

Feeling amused means you find something funny! We're often amused when something silly happens.

When you feel amused, you're likely smiling or laughing. You have a joyful, **excited** feeling in your body. Feeling amused is great. When you're amused, you're happy!

GOOFY AND GIGGLING

Alex's sister Kayla was putting on a show for the family. She hid behind a chair and held up two puppets.

Kayla pretended the puppets were singing in loud, **goofy** voices 😆. Alex couldn't stop laughing 😂! He rolled all around, **giggling**.

HOW DOES IT FEEL?

What does amusement feel like? It might be a happy, bubbling feeling in your belly.

It might be a smile tugging at the corners of your mouth. It might be a laugh that you just can't hold back.

LAUGH WITH, NOT AT

Jonah and Toby are best friends. They love to make each other laugh 😁! Laughing together makes them feel closer than ever.

One day Toby tripped and fell. Jonah laughed. He thought it looked silly! But Toby felt mad 😡.

Toby was **embarrassed** about falling. He didn't like being laughed at.

Jonah told Toby he was sorry 😔. He likes laughing *with* his friend. He doesn't want to laugh *at* him. It's not okay to be amused at someone else's **expense**.

YOUR SENSE OF HUMOR

What makes you smile? Maybe you like knock-knock jokes, but your brother doesn't. That's okay!

What you find amusing might be different from what somebody else does. Everybody has their own sense of humor, or idea of what's funny.

WHAT'S SO FUNNY?

Mai watched her grandpa read the newspaper. Grandpa had a little smile on his face 😊.

"What's so funny, Grandpa?" Mai asked. Grandpa showed Mai a **comic strip** in the newspaper. It showed a cat eating spaghetti. Grandpa **smirked** 😏.

"I don't get it," Mai said 😕. She looked and looked at the comic. She wasn't amused.

"That's all right, sweetheart," Grandpa said. He winked at Mai 😉.

"I like what I like. You like what you like!"

FINDING WHAT'S FUN

Maybe you're wondering how you can feel amused. Amusement often happens when we feel **relaxed** and happy.

Most of all, it happens when we're paying attention. Take time to notice what's going on around you. Chances are, you'll find something amusing!

WORDS TO KNOW

comic strip: One part of a cartoon's story printed in a book, newspaper, magazine, or online.

embarrassed: Feeling uncomfortable or unhappy.

excited: Having strong or lively feelings about something.

expense: At the cost of another's feelings.

giggle: To laugh.

goofy: Silly.

relaxed: Calm.

smirk: To give a small smile.

FOR MORE INFORMATION

BOOKS

Regan, Lisa. *Knock Knock Joke Book*. New York, NY: Windmill Books, 2020.

Wood, John. *Harry the Hamster Feels Happy*. New York, NY: Windmill Books, 2020.

WEBSITES

Fun Brain
www.funbrain.com
Explore lots of amusing games, videos, and books on Fun Brain!

Funology
www.funology.com
Try out fun crafts, games, jokes, and activities on this fun site.

Publisher's note to educators and parents: Our editors have carefully reviewed these websites to ensure that they are suitable for students. Many websites change frequently, however, and we cannot guarantee that a site's future contents will continue to meet our high standards of quality and educational value. Be advised that students should be closely supervised whenever they access the internet.

INDEX